quarantine quisine

recipes by Grace Ubben
photography by Isabel Sanchez

ISBN 978-0-578-73811-6

acknowledgements

First and foremost, we would like to thank our parents for encouraging us to dream big and supporting us in every endeavor. Thank you for letting us quarantine with you at home and for being our most willing taste testers throughout this project.

This book was a labor of love, and it wouldn't have been possible without the tremendous belief and support of our fabulous editor, Serena Moyle, without whom there would be no finished book in your hands.

We would also like to express our special thanks to Erin Pace for her able guidance and support in making this book look and feel beautiful. As always, she takes everything she touches up a couple notches!

And a heartfelt thank you to all of our family and friends. It definitely takes a village, and we're so thankful for everyone who supported us along the way and helped us get this book to the finish line.

Hi, we're Grace and Isabel.

We met while studying at the University of Florida (Go Gators!) and like many 2020 college grads, we found ourselves unemployed and confronting a global pandemic. Instead of falling into the quarantine slump, we put our love for food and photography together to create this cookbook. Throughout college, we have supported each other's passions as they developed, and now seemed like the perfect time to fully pursue them!

Grace's heart is in the kitchen. Nothing brings her more joy than creating a delicious meal for the people she loves. Throughout college, Grace developed a passion for creating healthy recipes, which she shares regularly on her Instagram account @deliciouslygraced, and using food as natural and holistic medicine to heal the body.

Isabel feels most comfortable, happy, and alive behind a camera. During her time in college, she has owned and operated a photography business dedicated to finding the beauty in the simplest things. Whether commemorating recent graduates, traveling the world, or enjoying a delicious meal, she knows how to capture the moment.

We decided to bring our talents together to create this book. Inside, you will find healthy and wholesome recipes that can be made with a few simple ingredients. We believe that home cooking is for everyone, so throw away that self-doubt – this is your moment to shine in the kitchen. Don't let the quarantine blues get you down. Put on your apron, wash your hands, and let's get cooking!

grace
+
isabel

PANTRY STAPLES

*These are the staples I keep stocked in my pantry to "healthify" a recipe,
whether its a batch of cookies or a smoothie.*

Almond Butter

Natural almond butter made from raw or roasted almonds contains nearly three times as much vitamin E, twice as much iron, and seven times as much calcium as peanut butter.

Chia Seeds

Chia seeds, high in plant-based protein and omega-3 fatty acids, deliver a massive amount of nutrients with very few calories. A perfect addition to smoothies, oatmeal, and more.

Almond Flour

Almond flour is my favorite alternative to traditional wheat flour. It's gluten-free, low in carbs, packed with nutrients and has a slightly sweeter taste.

Coconut Oil

Coconut oil is highly resistant to oxidation at high heat, making it suitable for high-heat cooking methods like frying. It's a great substitute for butter in baking, but will lend a subtle coconut taste to your recipe.

Cacao Powder

I always choose cacao powder over unsweetened cocoa powder whenever possible. Unlike cocoa, cacao powder is a minimally processed form of the bean that maintains the nutritionally dense properties of the cacao seed. And it's a delicious low-sugar chocolate.

Coconut Sugar

I try to avoid adding refined sugar to my cooking as much as possible. Coconut sugar is my favorite refined sugar substitute. It's low on the glycemic index and loaded with antioxidants and fiber that will allow you to enjoy your baked treats guilt-free.

Extra Virgin Olive Oil

Extra virgin olive oil is my go-to oil for stewing, sauteing, frying and baking. A classic, healthy choice for almost everything, full of antioxidants and unsaturated fats.

Ground Flax Seeds

This is truly the hidden gem in my pantry. Add a spoonful of ground flax seeds to smoothies, oatmeal, pancakes, or any baked goods for an unsuspecting omega-3 boost. It can also be used to make flax eggs, the perfect vegan-friendly egg alternative.

Raw Honey

Raw honey is a great refined sugar replacement. It's lower in fructose and absorbed more slowly by the body than refined sugar. This means longer-lasting energy and slightly less of a spike in blood sugar, which is easier on your body and digestive system.

Pure Maple Syrup

Pure maple syrup is the ultimate sweetener I keep in my kitchen to replace sugar. It's not only delicious, but also healthier than any other sweetener. Loaded with antioxidants, prebiotics and vitamins, maple syrup is a great topping on any sweet treat.

Oats

Oats make an easy, balanced breakfast packed with fiber and protein. The varieties I keep stocked in my pantry are old-fashioned rolled oats, steel-cut oats, and quick cooking oats.

Peanut Butter

Natural peanut butter made with only roasted peanuts and salt is a great, balanced energy source that supplies your body with protein, fiber, and healthy fats. Delicious and versatile, it's easily added to your smoothies, baked goods, or peanut sauce for a stir fry.

Protein Powder

Plant-based protein powder is a must-have in my pantry. It is the perfect addition to any smoothie recipe for extra benefits after a workout or a quick breakfast. I like to have both a vanilla and chocolate flavor to switch it up.

Pure Vanilla Extract

Adding vanilla extract to sweet baked goods mirrors the role salt plays when added to savory dishes by enhancing the other flavors in the recipe. I like to use pure vanilla extract that is free of any alcohol.

INGREDIENT SWAPS

*The following substitutions can be applied to any recipe in this book
to meet all taste preferences and dietary restrictions.*

Rice

For more flavorful rice, substitute half the water for chicken broth
and boil rice with 1-2 tablespoons of chopped scallions.

Nut Butter

If you're not a fan of peanut butter or almond butter, you can always
replace it with your favorite nut butter. Some great alternatives
include cashew butter, sunflower seed butter, coconut butter or
tahini.

Oil

If you don't like the strong taste of coconut oil, swap it out for
another neutral oil. Some great options include avocado oil,
sunflower oil, or canola oil.

Milk

Any of the recipes that call for milk can be made dairy-free and
vegan-friendly by swapping out dairy milk for your favorite plant-
based milk. Some great alternatives include almond milk, coconut
milk, oat milk, cashew milk and soy milk.

Yogurt

Any of the recipes that call for Greek yogurt can be made dairy-free and vegan-friendly by swapping out Greek yogurt for your favorite plant-based yogurt. Some great alternatives include almond-based yogurt, coconut yogurt or soy yogurt.

Egg

My favorite egg replacement is what I call the 'flax egg.' Mix together one tablespoon ground flaxseed meal with three tablespoons water. Let that mixture sit in the fridge for 15 minutes to set and thicken. After 15 minutes you'll notice that it's nice and goopy, just like an egg. Use in any recipes to replace an egg and make the recipe vegan-friendly.

Protein Powder

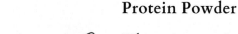

When using protein powder, you can use a whey protein or a casein protein powder. If you are looking for a dairy-free or vegan-friendly option, use a plant-based protein powder. Some of my favorites include pea protein, hemp protein, and brown rice protein.

Chocolate

Another easy way to make a sweets recipe vegan-friendly is by using dairy-free chocolate chips instead of traditional chocolate chips. You can find them in the baking section of your local grocery store. It's an easy swap that tastes just as sweet and delicious. If you can't find the chips, simply chop up a dairy-free chocolate bar instead.

Sweetener

There are many options for naturally sweetening your dishes. I prefer pure maple syrup or raw honey, but you can also use stevia, monk fruit, or your choice of sweetener.

RECIPES

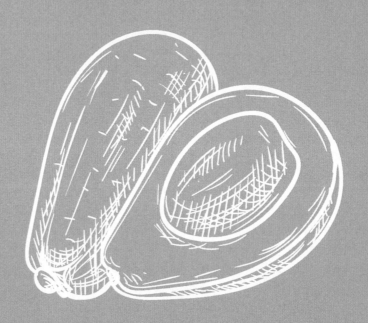

BREAKFAST

EASY LIKE SUNDAY MORNING PANCAKES

Quarantine feels a lot like groundhog day, living the same day over and over again – but it doesn't have to! While it may be easier to reach for boxed pancakes, I used my newfound free time to master these fluffy, homemade pancakes. A perfect addition to your Sunday morning Zoom brunch.

SERVES 6 | PREP TIME: 10 MINS | COOK TIME: 10 MINS

PREPARATION

In a large bowl, combine the flour, sugar, baking powder and salt. In a small bowl, combine the egg, milk, butter and vanilla extract. Add the wet ingredients to the dry ingredients and gently fold until well-combined, but still slightly lumpy. The batter should be thick, but easily pourable. Careful not to over-mix the batter or the pancakes could end up less fluffy. Set the batter aside to rest.

Heat a non-stick pan or griddle over medium-low heat. Melt a little butter on the pan to grease it. Pour batter onto the pan and let it spread out into a round pancake shape; about 3 tablespoons of batter per pancake. Allow batter to cook until bubbles appear on the surface and the edges are set; flip and cook until golden-brown. Re-grease the pan and continue this process with the remaining batter. Serve pancakes with maple syrup or your choice of toppings.

INGREDIENTS

2 cups all-purpose flour
4 Tablespoons sugar
4 teaspoons baking powder
1/2 teaspoon salt
1 large egg
1 & 1/2 cups milk of choice
4 Tablespoons butter, melted and slightly cooled
2 teaspoons vanilla extract

Optional toppings:
Banana slices
Blueberries
Chocolate chips

GREEN GODDESS BREKKY TACOS

Pajamas all day? Waking up late? Tacos for breakfast? Why not! Start your morning… or afternoon… with some dinner for breakfast! Bell pepper, arugula and cilantro add a gorgeous pop of color and an extra boost of macronutrients. But the best part… you won't feel so out of sync eating breakfast at noon.

SERVES 4 | PREP TIME: 10 MINS | COOK TIME: 10 MINS

PREPARATION

In a small nonstick skillet, heat 1 tablespoon of extra virgin olive oil over medium heat. Add the green pepper, scallions and a pinch of salt and pepper to the skillet. Sauté until lightly browned, about 5 minutes. Add a large spoonful of salsa to the skillet and stir. Remove from heat and set aside.

In a new, large, nonstick skillet, heat the remaining 1 tablespoon of olive oil over medium heat. Add the beaten eggs to the skillet and stir until partially cooked, about 10 seconds. Add the green pepper mixture to the eggs, stirring to combine. Remove skillet from the heat while the eggs are still slightly runny. Add the arugula/spinach and cilantro to the eggs, stir, and set aside.

To assemble the tacos, scoop 1/2 cup of the egg mixture, a spoonful of salsa, and a few slices of avocado onto a warmed tortilla. Finish with a squeeze of lime and a pinch of salt and pepper. Serve with lime wedges.

NOTES

For an even heartier brekky taco, top with shredded cheese, mix in black beans, and finish with guac and sour cream.

INGREDIENTS

2 Tablespoons extra virgin olive oil
1 green pepper, diced
3 scallions, chopped
Sea salt
Black pepper
Salsa, store-bought
6 eggs, beaten
2 cups arugula or spinach, chopped
1/4 cup cilantro, chopped
1 avocado, sliced
Lime wedges, for serving
8 tortillas, warmed

DAIRY-FREE
VEGETARIAN

GARDEN VEGGIE FRITTATA

Do you find yourself wandering the vegetable aisles of the grocery store, picking up every brightly colored veggie with the ideal plan of eating them all? Then like me, that makes you a "veggie idealist." Fear not! This recipe is perfect for clearing out the veggie drawer in your fridge. And besides, it's fun to say 'frittata'!

SERVES 4 | PREP TIME: 5 MINS | COOK TIME: 30 MINS

PREPARATION

Preheat oven to 350°F with a rack in the center position. In a large bowl, beat eggs with milk, salt and pepper and set aside. Next, warm the olive oil in a 10-inch ovenproof skillet over medium heat. Add red bell pepper and red onion to the skillet and sauté until softened, about 7 minutes. Add spinach to the skillet and sauté until wilted, about 2 minutes.

Distribute the vegetables evenly in the skillet and pour the egg mixture on top. Sprinkle with the crumbled feta cheese. Without stirring, allow the eggs to cook on the stove until they are just beginning to set around the edges, 2 to 3 minutes, then place the skillet in the oven.

Bake the frittata until almost set in the center, about 15 minutes. Broil the frittata on high until the top is golden brown, about 2 minutes, watching carefully to prevent over-browning. If the center still needs time to cook, but the top is browning, place a sheet of foil over the skillet. Remove from the oven. Let frittata rest for 5 minutes before serving.

NOTES

Substitute the veggies with whatever produce you have on hand. For an extra protein boost, add in chopped sausage, ground beef, or bacon.

INGREDIENTS

8 large eggs
1/3 cup milk
1/2 teaspoon salt
1/4 teaspoon pepper
2 Tablespoons extra virgin olive oil
1 medium red bell pepper, seeds removed, thinly sliced
1/2 cup red onion, thinly sliced
2 cups baby spinach, packed
4 ounces feta cheese

GLUTEN-FREE
VEGETARIAN

PEANUT BUTTER BANANA OATMEAL

The ultimate healthy breakfast recipe is here! This oatmeal will keep you full all morning long, putting the brakes on the need to reach for your stockpile of quarantine snacks. Plus, it's a great way to add more whole food ingredients into your diet.

SERVES 1 | PREP TIME: 5 MINS | COOK TIME: 5 MINS

PREPARATION

Bring 1 cup water to a boil in a medium pot. Stir in the old-fashioned oats, vanilla, cinnamon and a pinch of salt. Lower the heat to medium-low and simmer for 5 minutes, stirring occasionally.

Once the oats are fully cooked, scoop into a serving bowl. Top with peanut butter, banana slices, honey, chia seeds, and a pinch of cinnamon.

INGREDIENTS

Oatmeal:
1 cup water
1/2 cup old-fashioned oats
1/2 teaspoon vanilla extract
1/4 teaspoon cinnamon
Pinch of sea salt

Toppings:
1 Tablespoon peanut butter
1 banana, sliced
1 Tablespoon honey
Sprinkle of chia seeds
Pinch of cinnamon

DAIRY-FREE
VEGAN
VEGETARIAN

SOUTHWEST BREKKY QUESADILLA

It's no surprise that Tex-Mex ranks in the top 5 best comfort foods… and we could all use a little comfort after 2020! These protein and fiber-rich quesadillas are stuffed with scrambled eggs, black beans, fresh pico de gallo, and chipotle seasoning… did somebody say heaven?

SERVES 1 | PREP TIME: 5 MINS | COOK TIME: 5 MINS

PREPARATION

In a bowl, whisk the eggs with the chipotle seasoning until well blended. Add the black beans and set aside.

Heat a small skillet over medium heat. Spray with nonstick cooking spray. Pour the egg mixture and cook, stirring often, until the eggs are just set, about 2 minutes. Transfer the mixture to a bowl. Stir in the pico de gallo.

In a separate large skillet, warm the tortilla over medium heat, flipping occasionally. Once the pan and the tortilla are warm, sprinkle half the cheese over half of the tortilla. Top the cheese with scrambled eggs, then top the scrambled eggs with the remaining cheese. Fold the tortilla over the filling to cover. Let the quesadilla cook until golden and crispy on the bottom, about 1 to 2 minutes. Flip it and cook until the second side is golden and crispy.

Remove skillet from heat and transfer quesadilla to a cutting board. Let cool for a few minutes, then slice into 2 slices. Serve immediately with extra pico de gallo, lime juice, and cilantro.

INGREDIENTS

Nonstick cooking spray
1 large egg
1/8 - 1/4 teaspoon chipotle seasoning blend
2 Tablespoons canned black beans, drained and rinsed
2 Tablespoons pico de gallo, store-bought
1 flour tortilla
1/3 cup shredded Mexican blend cheese

Optional garnish:
Sour cream
Avocado
Salsa, store-bought

VEGETARIAN

EVERYDAY AVOCADO TOAST

Mashed avocado spread over crusty whole grain bread finished with a drizzle of olive oil, a pinch of red pepper flakes, and a fried egg—is your mouth watering yet? This classic recipe is full of healthy, unsaturated fats, packed with fiber, and will keep you energized all morning long. With one bite, you are sure to be converted into a true Millennial.

SERVES 1 | PREP TIME: 5 MINS | COOK TIME: 10 MINS

PREPARATION

Heat olive oil in a skillet over medium-low heat. Crack egg into the skillet and cook until white on the bottom and firm enough to flip, 2 to 3 minutes. Flip the egg, trying not to crack the yolk, and cook until egg reaches desired firmness, 2 to 5 minutes. Set egg aside.

While the bread toasts, in a small bowl, combine avocado, lime juice, salt, pepper, and red pepper flakes. Gently mash the avocado with the back of a fork to combine.

Top toasted bread with mashed avocado mixture and cooked egg. Drizzle with olive oil and top with a pinch of red pepper flakes.

INGREDIENTS

1/2 teaspoon extra virgin olive oil
1 egg
1 slice of bread, toasted
1/2 an avocado
1/2 teaspoon lime juice
1/8 teaspoon sea salt
1/8 teaspoon black pepper

Optional garnish:
Olive oil
Red pepper flakes

NOTES

The options are endless when it comes to topping your avocado toast. Get creative with the ingredients you have on hand! You can't go wrong with some sliced tomato, smoked salmon, roasted vegetables, or feta cheese.

DAIRY-FREE
VEGETARIAN

CLASSIC OVERNIGHT OATS

I can't be the only one who wakes up 15 minutes before their first Zoom meeting. Between throwing on a presentable shirt, and washing your face, grab these overnight oats to eat. Aren't you proud these were prepped the night before and stored in the fridge? Two claps for your efficiency.

SERVES 1 | PREP TIME: 5 MINS | REST TIME: OVERNIGHT

PREPARATION

Combine all ingredients in a bowl and pour into a mason jar or small glass container. Let sit in the fridge overnight. Add your favorite toppings in the morning when serving.

NOTES

Most people eat their overnight oats cold. If you prefer warm oats, heat them up in the microwave before serving.

INGREDIENTS

1/2 cup old-fashioned oats
1/3 cup plain Greek yogurt
1/3 cup milk of choice
1 teaspoon vanilla extract
1 Tablespoon maple syrup
Pinch of sea salt

Optional toppings:
Granola
Honey
Berries

VEGETARIAN

See next page for more.

OVERNIGHT OATS VARIATIONS

While the classic recipe is delicious, overnight oats can be customized in so many ways! Below are a few of my personal favorite combinations to inspire you. Simply follow the preparation instructions from the previous page, add some flavor options and enjoy!

Chocolate

Classic overnight oats recipe
1 & 1/2 Tablespoons cacao powder

Optional toppings:
Shredded coconut
Dark chocolate chips
Cacao powder

Cherry Garcia

Classic overnight oats recipe
Handful sliced almonds
Handful dried tart cherries

Optional toppings:
Granola
Honey
Fresh chopped cherries

Raspberry Banana

Classic overnight oats recipe
1/2 ripe banana, mashed
1/2 cup raspberries, mashed with a fork

Optional toppings:
Raspberries
Blueberries

Cinnamon Apple

Classic overnight oats recipe
1/3 small apple, diced
1 teaspoon cinnamon

Optional toppings:
Diced apple
Pinch of cinnamon

SMOOTHIES & SNACKS

VERY BERRY ANTIOXIDANT SMOOTHIE

This smoothie is a superfood in a cup! The antioxidant rich berries, high protein almond butter and healthy fats from the Greek yogurt make for an invigorating and powerful smoothie. Just the boost you need on those slower days at home.

SERVES 1 | PREP TIME: 5 MINS

PREPARATION

Place all ingredients in a high-powered blender. Blend on high for 1-2 minutes or until well- combined. Pour into a cup and enjoy.

INGREDIENTS

1 cup frozen mixed berries
1 frozen banana
1/4 cup plain Greek yogurt
1 Tablespoon almond butter
1 cup milk of choice

GLUTEN-FREE
VEGETARIAN

POWER GREEN SMOOTHIE

Most of us struggle to eat enough green veggies. Instead of fighting a losing battle with salads, make yourself a green smoothie. Side note: don't be afraid to use the cauliflower. It is nearly tasteless and gives your drink the perfect creamy consistency. Enjoy after your next at-home workout.

SERVES 1 | PREP TIME: 5 MINS

PREPARATION

Place all ingredients in a high-powered blender. Blend on high for 1-2 minutes or until well-combined. This may take a little extra time to get the spinach leaves fully broken down. Add more ice until the desired consistency is met. Pour into a cup and enjoy.

INGREDIENTS

1 frozen banana
1/2 cup frozen mango chunks
1 & 1/2 cups spinach
3 frozen cooked cauliflower florets
1 scoop of protein powder
1 Tablespoon peanut butter
1 cup milk of choice
Ice as needed

GLUTEN-FREE
VEGETARIAN

GOLDEN MILK SMOOTHIE

Golden milk originates from Ayurveda, an ancient branch of medicine in India. Originally a nourishing herbal drink, golden milk is still popular today under contemporary names like 'turmeric latte'. This smoothie is inspired by the restorative ingredients of golden milk and comes packed with anti-inflammatory properties to help your body recover faster.

SERVES 1 | PREP TIME: 5 MINS

PREPARATION

Place all ingredients in a high-powered blender. Blend on high for 1-2 minutes or until well combined. Pour into a cup and enjoy.

NOTES

Swap the frozen mango for frozen pineapple, or use a mixture of both!

INGREDIENTS

1 cup frozen mango chunks
1/2 frozen banana
1/2 cup plain Greek yogurt
1/2 teaspoon ground cinnamon
1/2 teaspoon ground turmeric
1/4 teaspoon ground ginger
1 cup milk of choice
Pinch of black pepper

GLUTEN-FREE
VEGETARIAN

COLD BREW COFFEE SMOOTHIE

Something about the repetitive routine of staying home day after day seems to suck the energy out of me. Two sips of this strong and nourishing beverage and I'm motivated to power through my to-do list.

SERVES 1 | PREP TIME: 5 MINS

PREPARATION

Place all ingredients in a high-powered blender. Blend on high for 1-2 minutes or until well combined. If necessary, add in more milk to thin the smoothie. Pour into a cup and enjoy.

INGREDIENTS

1/4 cup cold brew coffee
1 frozen banana
1 teaspoon vanilla extract
1 Tablespoon peanut butter
1/2 cup ice
1/2 cup milk of choice
1/2 Tablespoon cacao powder (or unsweetened cocoa powder)
1 Tablespoon maple syrup
1 serving protein powder (optional)

GLUTEN-FREE
VEGETARIAN

LEMONY BEETROOT HUMMUS

Can somebody say Instagram-worthy?! This gorgeous beetroot hummus was born ready for a photo-op. Your life may not be filled with instagram-able moments right now, but this hummus is sure to be the star of your palette and your IG feed.

SERVES 4 | PREP TIME: 10 MINS

PREPARATION

Place beets, chickpeas, garlic, lemon juice, tahini, olive oil, and salt into a high powered blender or food processor. Blend or pulse until smooth and creamy. Taste and adjust seasoning, if needed.

Transfer hummus to a serving bowl. Sprinkle with fresh parsley, sesame seeds, chickpeas, and drizzle with olive oil. Enjoy with veggie sticks, crackers, or homemade pita chips.

NOTES

You can find pre-cooked beets at your local grocery store. This saves you a ton of time and hassle, making this recipe super easy to throw together in just a matter of minutes! However, the color will not turn out quite as vibrant.

INGREDIENTS

2 medium beets, cooked
1 can chickpeas, drained and rinsed
2 garlic cloves, minced
Juice of 2 lemons
1/4 cup tahini
1/4 cup extra virgin olive oil
1 teaspoon sea salt

Toppings:
Handful of fresh parsley, chopped
1 teaspoon sesame seeds
Handful of chickpeas
1 Tablespoon extra virgin olive oil

GLUTEN-FREE
DAIRY-FREE
VEGAN
VEGETARIAN

HOMEMADE PITA CHIPS

Sometimes you just need a pita chip that's crunchy on the outside and soft on the inside. This simple, five-ingredient recipe is ready in 10 minutes flat and is the perfect compliment to your beetroot hummus.

SERVES 2 | PREP TIME: 3 MINS | COOK TIME: 8 MINS

PREPARATION

Preheat oven to 350°F. Without opening the pita pockets, cut them into triangles and place in a single layer on a baking sheet.

In a small bowl, mix the olive oil, Italian seasoning, garlic, and sea salt. Brush the pita triangles on both sides with the olive oil mixture.

Bake for 4 minutes on each side for crunchy pita chips with a slight softness on the inside. Bake longer for extra crunchy pita chips.

INGREDIENTS

2 pita pockets, store-bought
2 Tablespoons extra virgin olive oil
1 teaspoon Italian seasoning
2 garlic cloves, minced
Pinch of sea salt

DAIRY-FREE
VEGAN
VEGETARIAN

CLASSIC CHIA PUDDING

Chia pudding is my favorite wholesome replacement for processed snacks. It's high in fiber, protein, and healthy fats that are beneficial for controlling blood sugar, maintaining gut health and building lean muscle. It deserves the highest praise!

SERVES 1 | PREP TIME: 5 MINS | REST TIME: OVERNIGHT

PREPARATION

In a small bowl, mix all ingredients together. Leave on the counter at room temperature for 15 minutes to thicken. Once thick, stir again and add an extra splash of milk if too thick.

Cover and refrigerate overnight (or at least 6 hours). Before serving, stir in your favorite toppings and enjoy!

NOTES

Store chia pudding in the fridge for up to a week and grab one when you're hungry.

INGREDIENTS

3 Tablespoons chia seeds
1 Tablespoon maple syrup
1 teaspoon vanilla extract
3/4 cup milk of choice

GLUTEN-FREE
VEGETARIAN

See next page for more.

CHIA PUDDING VARIATIONS

Below are my favorite spins on the classic chia pudding recipe! Simply follow the same preparation instructions mentioned on the previous page using these new flavor options.

Banana Bread

3 Tablespoons chia seeds
1/2 banana, mashed
1/2 teaspoon ground cinnamon
3/4 cup milk of choice

Optional garnishes:
Walnuts, chopped
1/2 a banana, sliced

Lemon Raspberry

3 Tablespoons chia seeds
1 Tablespoon maple syrup
Zest of 1 lemon
2/3 cup milk of choice
1/4 cup fresh raspberries, mashed

Optional garnishes:
Blueberries
Honey
Granola

Dark Chocolate

3 Tablespoons chia seeds
2 Tablespoons cacao powder
2 Tablespoons maple syrup
3/4 cup milk of choice

Optional garnishes:
Yogurt
Hazelnuts, chopped
Chocolate chips

Strawberries & Cream

3 Tablespoons chia seeds
1 Teaspoon vanilla extract
1/4 cup full fat coconut milk
1/2 cup milk of choice
2 Tablespoons strawberry jam

Optional garnishes:
Strawberries, sliced
Almonds, slivered

CLASSIC NO-BAKE ENERGY BITES

It may seem strange for a recipe to use instant and regular oats but trust me on this… Blending the two types of oats makes these much easier to roll and shape into perfect energy bites. In minutes you will have a budget-friendly, whole food snack ready to pop in your mouth and eat. Roll away!

SERVES 12 | PREP TIME: 15 MINS | REST TIME: 60 MINS

PREPARATION

In a medium bowl, mix all ingredients until fully combined. The mixture should be sticky. Refrigerate for at least 30 minutes.

After chilling, spoon about a tablespoon of the mixture into your hand, roll into a ball, and place on a baking sheet. Repeat until all of the mixture has been used; about 12 energy bites.

Place the baking sheet in the freezer for about 30 minutes to set. Remove from the freezer and enjoy!

NOTES

To store, simply place the energy bites in an airtight container or in ziplock bags. Keep in the fridge for up to a week. Freezes well.

INGREDIENTS

Base Recipe:
1/2 cup old-fashioned oats
1/2 cup quick cooking oats
1/4 cup peanut butter or almond butter
1/4 cup honey or maple syrup
1/2 teaspoon vanilla extract
1 Tablespoon chia seeds
Pinch of sea salt, optional

GLUTEN-FREE
DAIRY-FREE
VEGAN
VEGETARIAN

See next page for more.

ENERGY BITE VARIATIONS

Not only do these energy bites taste like dessert, but they are super customizable. Below are some of my favorite flavor combinations. Start with the base recipe from the previous page and add these mix-ins for a variety of flavor options! Your snack game will never be the same.

Double Chocolate

Base recipe (using peanut butter)
2 Tablespoons cacao powder
1/2 cup mini chocolate chips

Carrot Cake

Base recipe (using almond butter)
1/4 cup shredded coconut
1 cup finely shredded carrots
1/2 teaspoon ground cinnamon

Oatmeal Raisin

Base recipe (using almond butter)
1/4 cup raisins
1/4 cup chopped pecans
1/2 teaspoon ground cinnamon

Trail Mix

Base recipe (using peanut butter)
1/4 cup dry roasted peanuts
1/4 cup mini M&M's
1/4 cup mini chocolate chips

White Chocolate Cranberry

Base recipe (using almond butter)
1/4 cup dried cranberries
1/4 cup white chocolate chips

Cashew Ginger

Base recipe (using almond butter)
1/4 cup crystallized ginger chopped
1/2 cup cashews chopped
1/2 teaspoon ground cinnamon
1/2 teaspoon ground ginger

MEALS

STEAK TACOS WITH AVOCADO ORANGE SALSA

It's time to elevate your quarantine dinner game above your go-to boxed mac and cheese. Yes, you… I'm calling you out. If you want to remind yourself what it was like to eat tacos from your favorite fast-casual restaurant, start with juicy, grilled ribeye and end with a tangy avocado orange salsa.

SERVES 4-6 | PREP TIME: 50 MINS | COOK TIME: 10 MINS

PREPARATION

Begin by mixing all of the steak marinade ingredients in a small bowl. Brush the marinade onto the ribeye and chill in the refrigerator for 15 minutes. For a stronger flavor, marinate the steak overnight.

While the steak is marinating, combine the navel oranges, red bell pepper, red onion, cilantro, lime juice, jalapeño, garlic and salt in a large bowl and stir. Chill for 30-60 minutes.

To cook on the grill, heat your grill to medium heat and place the ribeye on the grill. To cook on the stove, heat a large frypan over medium-high heat and place the ribeye on the frypan. Cook according to your preference. Recommended 3 minutes per side for medium. Once cooked, set aside to rest. Lightly coat the tortillas with cooking spray and grill 1-2 minutes on each side and set aside.

Before assembling tacos and serving, add the diced avocado to the salsa. Slice the ribeye into thin pieces and place on warmed tortilla. Top with a generous spoonful of avocado orange salsa.

INGREDIENTS

1 & 1/2 lbs thick-cut ribeye
12 flour tortillas

Steak marinade:
4 Tablespoons extra virgin olive oil
4 teaspoons soy sauce
2 teaspoons sea salt
1 teaspoon black pepper
1 teaspoon cayenne pepper
2 Tablespoons brown sugar
4 cloves garlic, minced

Avocado Orange Salsa:
2 cups navel oranges, peeled and diced
1/2 cup red bell pepper, diced
1/2 cup red onion, minced
2 Tablespoons cilantro, chopped
1 & 1/2 Tablespoons lime juice
1 Tablespoon jalapeño, seeded and minced
1 teaspoon garlic, minced
1/4 teaspoon sea salt
1 avocado, diced

CHICKEN TORTILLA SOUP

Fall is approaching and though the leaves change and your garden wilts, quarantine remains the same. As the temperature drops, this is my go-to cozy meal for the cooler months. The best part of this seasonal change: your sweatpants can now be excused as 'weather-appropriate.'

SERVES 4-6 | PREP TIME: 10 MINS | COOK TIME: 20 MINS

PREPARATION

In a large saucepan, heat the olive oil over medium-high heat. Add the onions and sauté until translucent, about 3 minutes. Add the garlic and jalapeños and cook for an additional minute. Add the chicken broth, tomatoes and beans to the saucepan and bring to a boil. Once at a boil, lower the heat to a simmer. [Puree with a stick blender at this point if you prefer your soup less chunky.]

Add raw chicken breasts to the simmering soup. Allow the chicken to cook for 8-10 minutes. Once fully cooked, remove from the soup, shred, and set aside.

Finish off soup with lime juice and cilantro. To serve, place a mound of shredded chicken in a bowl and ladle the soup over the chicken. Top with a squeeze of fresh lime juice, shredded cheese, tortilla strips, or croutons.

INGREDIENTS

2 Tablespoons extra virgin olive oil
1 small onion, diced
2 Tablespoons garlic, minced
1 jalapeño, seeded and minced
6 cups chicken broth
1 can fire roasted diced tomatoes
1 can black beans, drained and rinsed
3 chicken breasts
Juice of 1 lime
1 cup cilantro, chopped

Optional garnish:
Lime juice
Baked tortilla strips
Shredded Mexican blend cheese
Croutons

NOTES

Use 2 jalapenos for a spicier kick.

GLUTEN-FREE
DAIRY-FREE

LOADED VEGGIE BURRITO BOWL

Have you heard? The word burrito can now be used as a verb! Example: "I spent the day 'burritoed' on the couch." In fact, it's frowned upon to not spend your time burritoed on the couch during quarantine. Match your food to your mood and make this loaded veggie burrito bowl! You may feel guilty about your sedentary lifestyle, but you won't feel guilty about eating this plant-based, naturally vegan and gluten-free meal.

SERVES 2 | PREP TIME: 5 MINS | COOK TIME: 10 MINS

PREPARATION

Heat a small saucepan over medium heat. Add black beans, tomatoes, and a pinch of salt to the pot and cook for 4-5 minutes, stirring often.

Heat olive oil in a medium saucepan over medium heat. Add diced red peppers to the saucepan and sauté for 5 minutes, until soft. Add frozen corn to the saucepan, stirring until corn is defrosted and warm. Season with paprika, chili powder, cumin, garlic powder, black pepper, and red pepper flakes.

To serve, fill the bottom of a bowl with rice and top with your black beans and sautéed veggies. Garnish with chopped cilantro and sliced avocado. For extra flavor, add one of the optional garnishes as a finishing touch.

INGREDIENTS

2 cups rice, cooked
1 can black beans, drained and rinsed
1/2 tomato, diced
Pinch of sea salt
1 Tablespoon extra virgin olive oil
2 red bell peppers, diced
1 cup frozen corn
1/2 teaspoon paprika
1/2 teaspoon chili powder
1/2 teaspoon cumin
1/2 teaspoon garlic powder
1/4 teaspoon black pepper
Pinch red pepper flakes
1/4 cup cilantro, chopped
1 avocado, sliced

Optional garnishes:
Salsa verde, store-bought
Cilantro lime dressing, store-bought
Jalapeño, thinly sliced
Hot sauce

GLUTEN-FREE
DAIRY-FREE
VEGAN
VEGETARIAN

CAULI RICE STUFFED PEPPERS

Cauliflower rice is trending, but few people know how to incorporate it into their meals. This twist on a classic recipe is one of my favorite ways to substitute a healthy ingredient. The bell peppers are loaded with vitamin C for an extra immune system boost—something we could all use these days.

SERVES 6 | PREP TIME: 20 MINS | COOK TIME: 60 MINS

PREPARATION

Preheat oven to 350°F. In a large skillet, heat olive oil over medium heat and sauté onion until soft. Add beef to the skillet and stir until browned. Add bag of cauliflower rice to the skillet and stir until fully cooked. Once cooked, add 1 can of tomato sauce, onion powder, garlic powder, salt, pepper, and Italian seasoning to the beef. Reduce heat to low and simmer.

Cut the bell peppers in half, removing the tops, seeds, and membranes. Arrange the peppers in a deep baking dish with the hollow side face-up.

Grab your ground beef mixture and fill each bell pepper to the top. Pour the remaining can of tomato sauce over the stuffed peppers and sprinkle with more Italian seasoning.

Cover the baking dish with aluminum foil and bake for 1 hour in the oven, or until the peppers are tender. About 10 minutes before finishing, remove the foil and top the peppers with shredded cheese. Remove from the oven and let cool a bit before serving.

INGREDIENTS

1 Tablespoon extra virgin olive oil
1 yellow onion, chopped
1 pound ground beef
1 bag of fresh cauliflower rice
6 bell peppers
2 cans tomato sauce
1/4 teaspoon garlic powder
1/4 teaspoon onion powder
2 teaspoons Italian seasoning
Sea salt and black pepper, to taste

Optional garnish:
1 cup shredded Mexican blend cheese

GLUTEN-FREE

CRUNCHY CURRY CHICKEN SALAD

Cooking from home during quarantine doesn't have to be boring. This curry chicken salad is the perfect way to spice up your lunch game. The blend of exotic curry spices, sweet raisins, and crunchy cashews make for a meal balanced in fat, fiber, and protein. Eating 'international' foods may be the closest we get to traveling this year.

SERVES 4 | PREP TIME: 10 MINS

PREPARATION

In a large bowl, stir together mayo, apple cider vinegar, curry powder, pepper and salt. Add shredded chicken, celery, raisins and red onion to the bowl. Stir until well combined. Taste and adjust seasoning, if needed.

Serve over a bed of greens, on bread as a sandwich, or in lettuce wraps. Top with chopped cashews.

NOTES

For quick and easy shredded chicken, there are two great options. Either boil raw chicken breasts in water for 8-10 minutes or buy a cooked rotisserie chicken at the grocery store.

INGREDIENTS

1/4 cup mayo
1 teaspoon apple cider vinegar
1/2 Tablespoon curry powder
1/4 teaspoon black pepper
1/8 teaspoon sea salt
2 cups cooked chicken, shredded
3/4 cup celery, chopped
1/4 cup raisins
1/4 cup red onion, chopped
2 Tablespoons cashews, chopped

GLUTEN-FREE
DAIRY-FREE

LEMON PESTO PASTA

I'm sure you jumped on the quarantine bandwagon and planted an herb garden. The question is: have you used any of your herbs yet? This lemon pesto pasta is the perfect opportunity to cook with your freshly grown basil. This bold and flavorful meal will give you an excuse to buy more plants!

SERVES 6 | PREP TIME: 10 MINS | COOK TIME: 20 MINS

PREPARATION

Preheat oven to 450°F. Lay your sliced tomato on a baking sheet and sprinkle with salt, pepper, and dried basil. Bake in oven for 15-20 minutes until lightly browned and roasted.

While the tomatoes are roasting, cook the penne pasta in a large pot according to package directions. 2 minutes before the pasta is done, add the baby broccoli to the same pot of pasta and cook for the remaining few minutes. The broccoli should turn bright green.

Drain the pasta and broccoli, preserving about 1/4 cup of the pasta water. Transfer pasta, broccoli and pasta water to a bowl. Return the empty pot to medium high heat. Add garlic to the pot and cook for 1-2 minutes, until fragrant. Add the pasta and broccoli, the pesto, half the feta cheese, and the lemon juice to the pot. Stir until well-combined. Remove from heat and stir in the basil ribbons. To serve, top with remaining feta and roasted tomatoes.

INGREDIENTS

1 large tomato, sliced
Pinch of sea salt
Pinch of black pepper
Pinch of dried basil
18 ounces penne pasta
2 cups baby broccoli
2 cloves garlic, minced
1/2 cup pesto, store-bought
1/2 cup feta cheese
Juice of 2 lemons
Fresh basil, cut into ribbons

VEGETARIAN

PESCARITOS

I'm going to let you in on a little family secret. My dad hates the name 'fish tacos.' According to him, the only true tacos are beef tacos. Sad, I know. So a couple years ago, we decided to rebrand fish tacos as Pescaritos! Now, it's just as much fun to say as it is to eat. This recipe combines smoky spices, colorful slaw, and a squeeze of lime juice, all wrapped up in a warm tortilla. These tacos are easy, fresh, and delicious... and my dad loves them!

SERVES 4 | PREP TIME: 20 MINS | COOK TIME: 15 MINS

PREPARATION

In a large bowl, combine the coleslaw mix, cilantro, lime juice, honey, salt and pepper. Add additional lime juice or honey to taste. Set aside to rest, allowing the salt and lime juice to soften the cabbage.

Place the fish in a shallow dish (or ziplock bag) and pat dry with a paper towel. Doing so will help the seasoning stick to the fish. In a small bowl, combine the chili powder, cumin, garlic powder, onion powder, smoked paprika, and salt. Rub down the fish with the seasoning blend, coating generously.

In a large skillet, warm the olive oil over medium heat. Place the fish in the skillet and cook 3-4 minutes per side or until fish is opaque. Remove fish from the skillet and gently separate into small pieces.

To assemble your tacos, spoon the slaw and fish onto a warm tortilla. Garnish with your favorite extras, such as avocado slices, additional cilantro, and a spoonful of salsa.

INGREDIENTS

For the slaw:
4 cups coleslaw mix, store-bought
1/4 cup cilantro, chopped
Juice of 1 lime
1/2 Tablespoon honey
1/4 teaspoon sea salt
1/4 teaspoon black pepper

For the fish:
1 & 1/2 lbs. tilapia or cod, thawed if frozen
2 teaspoons chili powder
1/2 teaspoon cumin
1/2 teaspoon garlic powder
1/2 teaspoon onion powder
1/2 teaspoon smoked paprika
1/2 teaspoon sea salt
2 Tablespoons extra virgin olive oil

To serve:
8 tortillas, warmed
1 avocado, sliced
Fresh cilantro, chopped
Salsa, store-bought

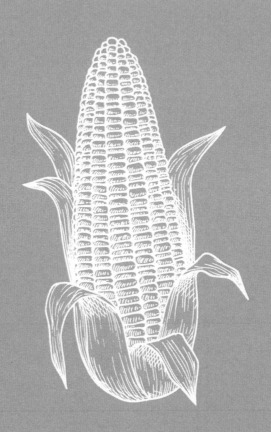

SALADS & SIDES

CORN & FETA SALAD

We've all been doing a bit more daydreaming during quarantine, fantasizing about where we'll go when we're not stuck at home. Well, just one bite of this summery salad and you will be instantly transported to the tropical getaway of your dreams. Just don't get mad at me when you have to come back to reality!

SERVES 4 | PREP TIME: 10 MINS | REST TIME: 60 MINS

PREPARATION

Bring a large pot of salted water to a boil. Add corn and cook 5 minutes. Drain corn and season with salt and pepper. Remove corn kernels from the cob and chill for 30-60 minutes in the fridge.

In a large mixing bowl, combine corn, diced tomato, chopped red onion, and sweet peppers. Drizzle olive oil and lime juice over the veggies and toss to coat. Add cilantro, salt, and pepper to taste. Top with crumbled feta cheese and serve chilled.

NOTES

For quick and easy corn, use 2 cans of sweet corn or a thawed bag of frozen corn.

INGREDIENTS

5 ears corn
1 tomato, seeded and diced
1/4 red onion, chopped
1 cup mini sweet peppers, diced
3 Tablespoons extra virgin olive oil
Juice of 1 lime
Cilantro, chopped
Pinch of sea salt
Pinch of black pepper
1/4 cup feta cheese

GLUTEN-FREE
VEGETARIAN

CAULI TABBOULEH SALAD

We could all take a note from the famed Mediterranean diet during the current pandemic. This recipe combines some of the classic Mediterranean staples into a refreshing and colorful salad full of antioxidants! Your immune system will thank you.

SERVES 4 | PREP TIME: 15 MINS

PREPARATION

Begin by preparing your cauliflower rice. Chop the head of cauliflower into florets and place in a food processor. Pulse for 10-15 seconds until the texture resembles rice. Place cauliflower rice in a large mixing bowl with cucumber, cherry tomatoes, red onion, mint, and parsley. Toss to combine.

In a small bowl, whisk together lemon juice, red wine vinegar, and olive oil. Optional: add basil, salt and lemon pepper to the dressing.

Pour the dressing over the vegetable mixture and toss to coat. Serve immediately or refrigerate to let the flavors meld together before serving.

NOTES

For added convenience, substitute the head of cauliflower with a bag of fresh cauliflower rice. Just make sure it is fresh, not frozen. You will need 3-4 cups. Top this off with some feta cheese, kalamata olives, and chicken breast for some extra mediterranean flavor and protein!

INGREDIENTS

1 large head cauliflower
1 cup cucumber, chopped
3/4 cup cherry tomatoes, chopped
1/3 cup red onion, chopped
1/3 cup fresh mint, chopped
1/3 cup fresh parsley, chopped
Juice of 1 lemon
1 Tablespoon red wine vinegar
2 Tablespoons extra virgin olive oil

Optional garnish:
1 teaspoon dried basil
Sea salt, to taste
Lemon pepper, to taste

GLUTEN-FREE
DAIRY-FREE
VEGAN
VEGETARIAN

WILD RICE, MANGO & BLACK BEAN SALAD

I know you panicked and stockpiled canned beans (and toilet paper!) when COVID struck. Fear not, I'm here to help you turn those beans into a masterpiece. This salad is a family favorite and crowd pleaser… save it for whenever we are allowed to gather in groups again or eat the entire bowl yourself!

SERVES 6 | PREP TIME: 5 MINS | COOK TIME: 45 MINS

PREPARATION

In a small saucepan, add the wild rice to 2 cups of water and bring to a boil. When the water boils, reduce the heat to simmer and cover for 45 minutes. Once the rice is tender, strain the remaining water and chill for 30-60 minutes.

Once chilled, place rice in a medium mixing bowl and fluff with a fork. Add the mango, black beans, green onions, cilantro, lime juice, olive oil, salt, and pepper to the bowl. Toss and serve.

NOTES

For added convenience, purchase prepared wild rice. Set aside seasoning packet.

INGREDIENTS

1/2 cup wild rice, dry
1 & 1/2 cups mango, chopped
1 can black beans, drained and rinsed
1 cup green onions, sliced
3 Tablespoons fresh cilantro, chopped
2 Tablespoons salsa, store-bought
2 Tablespoons lime juice
2 Tablespoons extra virgin olive oil
3/4 teaspoon sea salt
1/4 teaspoon black pepper

GLUTEN-FREE
DAIRY-FREE
VEGAN
VEGETARIAN

TOMATO & AVOCADO SALAD

Tomato and avocado salad is part crunchy, part creamy, and entirely what I crave when I want a healthy fix. A simple yet satisfying dish perfect for socially distanced picnics! Eat this on its own or dig in with some tortilla chips.

SERVES 4-6 | PREP TIME: 5 MINS | COOK TIME: 20 MINS

PREPARATION

In a large bowl, gently toss the tomatoes, cucumbers, avocado, and red onion.

In a separate small bowl, whisk together the ingredients for the dressing. Pour the dressing over the salad and toss to coat.

Let rest for 20 minutes, allowing the flavors to fully develop. Serve and enjoy!

NOTES

Some delicious, optional add-ins include feta cheese, fresh mozzarella cheese, olives, marinated artichoke hearts, and diced green pepper.

INGREDIENTS

4 tomatoes, chopped
2 cucumbers, chopped
2 avocados, diced
1/2 medium red onion, thinly sliced

Dressing:
1/4 cup extra virgin olive oil
Juice of 2 lemons
2 cloves garlic, minced
2 teaspoons dried oregano
1 teaspoon sea salt
1 teaspoon black pepper
4 Tablespoons fresh parsley, minced

GLUTEN-FREE
DAIRY-FREE
VEGAN
VEGETARIAN

WATERMELON FETA SALAD

Social distancing has encouraged a lot of us to spend more time outdoors. After a day on the beach or a walk through the neighborhood, this is a refreshing and hydrating salad. Low on calories but high in flavor, it's a win-win.

SERVES 4 | PREP TIME: 15 MINS

PREPARATION

In a large mixing bowl, add the watermelon, cucumber, red onion, feta cheese, and fresh herb(s) of choice; mint, basil, or cilantro. Gently toss to combine. Drizzle with lime juice. Add salt and pepper to taste. Gently toss again and serve immediately.

INGREDIENTS

4 cups watermelon, cubed
1/2 large cucumber, chopped
1/4 cup red onion, thinly sliced
1/3 cup feta cheese
2 Tablespoons fresh mint, basil, or cilantro, chopped
Juice of 1/2 lime
Sea salt, to taste
Black pepper, to taste

GLUTEN-FREE
VEGETARIAN

BAKED SWEET POTATO FRIES

Baked, not fried. Need I say more? If you aren't convinced yet, imagine homemade sweet potato fries made with minimal effort that taste both salty and sweet. You're welcome. Warning: you should probably make a double batch because these are highly addictive!

SERVES 4 | PREP TIME: 15 MINS | COOK TIME: 40 MINS

PREPARATION

Preheat oven to 425°F. Wrap the sweet potatoes in a dish towel and microwave for 5 minutes. Let cool for 1-2 minutes. Cut the sweet potatoes into wedges and place in a large mixing bowl.

In a small bowl, combine the garlic powder, paprika, salt, and cayenne pepper. Add olive oil and seasonings to sweet potato wedges, tossing gently until evenly coated.

Spread fries in a single layer on 2 baking sheets. Place in oven and bake 35-40 minutes, until crisp. Serve immediately and enjoy!

INGREDIENTS

2 large sweet potatoes
1 teaspoon garlic powder
2 teaspoons paprika
1 teaspoon sea salt
1/4 teaspoon cayenne pepper
2 Tablespoons extra virgin olive oil

GLUTEN-FREE
DAIRY-FREE
VEGAN
VEGETARIAN

CRISPY POTATOES & PARSLEY DRIZZLE

I will give you 10 seconds to name a food that is as versatile, delicious, and affordable as potatoes. Couldn't think of one? Me neither. While crispy potatoes may be a classic staple in many kitchens, this parsley dressing is a unique staple in mine. Try it on your baked chicken, beef tacos, or grilled salmon next!

SERVES 3 | PREP TIME: 5 MINS | COOK TIME: 40 MINS

PREPARATION

Preheat oven to 425°F. Evenly spread the potatoes, green pepper, and onion onto a baking sheet. Top with with olive oil, paprika, salt, and pepper and toss to coat.

Place in the oven and roast for 20 minutes. Avoid using parchment paper or aluminum foil, as this could cause the vegetables to steam rather than crisp up. After 20 minutes, toss the vegetables and bake for another 15-20 minutes until browned and crisp.

While the vegetables are roasting, place all of the Parsley Drizzle ingredients in a food processor and pulse until smooth. Drizzle over potatoes when serving.

NOTES

You can make a big batch of the Parsley Drizzle and store in your fridge for up to 4 weeks.

INGREDIENTS

Crispy Potatoes:
3 red potatoes, quartered
1 green pepper, chopped
1 small onion, chopped
1 teaspoon extra virgin olive oil
1/4 teaspoon paprika
Sea salt, to taste
Black pepper, to taste

Parsley Drizzle:
1/2 cup extra virgin olive oil
1/4 cup olive oil mayo
1/4 cup grated parmesan
1/2 cup chopped parsley
1 Tablespoon sugar
1 Tablespoon red wine vinegar
1 teaspoon sea salt
1 teaspoon black pepper
Juice of 1 lemon

VEGETARIAN

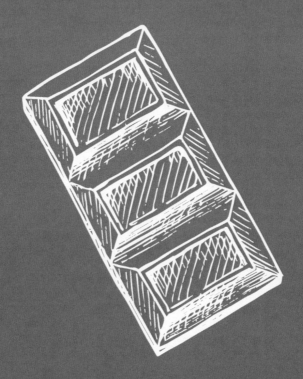

SWEETS

THE BEST BANANA BREAD

Do you have some overripe bananas sitting in your kitchen? Are you looking for an excuse to do some weekend baking? I'm here to tell you that this is THE banana bread recipe you have looked for all your life. Seriously. It is dense, moist, fluffy, and refined-sugar free… in other words, it's happiness in a pan. Cheers to that.

SERVES 8 | PREP TIME: 10 MINS | COOK TIME: 50 MINS

PREPARATION

Preheat oven to 350°F. Spray a loaf pan with nonstick cooking spray. In a large bowl, mix all the dry ingredients and set aside.

In a separate large bowl, use a fork to mash the bananas. Add the egg and stir to combine. Add the maple syrup, almond milk and vanilla extract and stir again to combine. Slowly add the dry ingredients to the wet ingredients, stirring continuously. Add the melted coconut oil to the batter and stir to combine.

Pour the batter into the loaf pan. Bake for 30 minutes, then cover with tin foil and bake for another 15-20 minutes. Let cool for 15 minutes, slice, and enjoy!

INGREDIENTS

Dry:
1 & 3/4 cups all-purpose flour
3/4 cup coconut sugar
2 teaspoons baking soda
1/8 teaspoon sea salt
1 teaspoon cinnamon

Wet:
1 egg
3 medium ripe bananas
1/4 cup maple syrup
1/2 cup almond milk
1 teaspoon vanilla extract
1/4 cup coconut oil, melted

Optional toppings:
Walnuts
Pecans
Pumpkin seeds
Sunflower seeds
Banana slices

DAIRY-FREE
VEGETARIAN

CHEWY CHOCOLATE CHIP COOKIES

I'm well aware that gluten-free desserts often get a bad rap, but I want you to stay open-minded about this one. This not-so-classic chocolate chip cookie recipe will give you the chewiest cookies you've baked yet. Perfect for those late-night cravings, easily replacing those refrigerated, calorie-laden, roll and bake types.

SERVES 12 | PREP TIME: 40 MINS | COOK TIME: 10 MINS

PREPARATION

Preheat oven to 350°F. Line a baking sheet with parchment paper.

In a medium bowl, mix the egg, coconut sugar, coconut oil, and maple syrup. Add the almond flour, baking soda, vanilla extract, and salt to the bowl and stir until a cookie dough is formed. Gently fold chocolate chips into the cookie dough. Refrigerate the dough for 20 minutes.

Once the dough has chilled, use a small ice cream scoop to create balls of dough. Dough balls should be on the smaller size because they will spread a bit while baking.

Place the dough balls two inches apart on the baking sheet and use your fingers to gently flatten. Bake for 8-10 minutes. Remove from the oven and let cool for 10 minutes before eating.

INGREDIENTS

1 egg
1/2 cup coconut sugar
3 Tablespoons coconut oil (or butter)
2 Tablespoons maple syrup
2 cups almond flour
1 teaspoon baking soda
1 teaspoon vanilla extract
1/2 teaspoon sea salt
1/3 cup chocolate chips

GLUTEN-FREE
VEGETARIAN

84

CHOCOLATE MUG CAKE

Living alone can be hard on one's sweet tooth, and baking an entire pan of brownies or batch of cupcakes is too much for one person. When you're quarantined alone and craving something sweet, this single-serve cake is the perfect treat for you! I'm digging in with you, in spirit.

SERVES 1 | PREP TIME: 5 MINS | COOK TIME: 2 MINS

PREPARATION

In a small bowl, whisk all the ingredients together. Pour the batter into a small 9-oz mug and microwave for 1-2 minutes, or until the cake is cooked through. Let cool for a couple of minutes before digging in.

If using an oven, bake in a 3-inch ramekin at 375°F for 20 minutes. Enjoy plain or top with whipped cream, powdered sugar and berries.

INGREDIENTS

1/4 cup almond flour
2 Tablespoons cacao powder
2 Tablespoons maple syrup
1 teaspoon coconut oil
1 teaspoon vanilla extract
1 large egg

Optional Toppings:
Whipped cream
Powdered sugar
Berries
Chocolate chips

GLUTEN-FREE
DAIRY-FREE
VEGETARIAN

86

COOKIE DOUGH FREEZER FUDGE

For those of us quarantining with family, hiding our favorite food from unwelcome nibblers is all too real. The next time you crave dessert, discreetly whip together this fudge and hide it in the back of the freezer. Be sure to pick a good spot… otherwise, this fudge will be gone in minutes!

SERVES 12 | PREP TIME: 5 MINS | REST TIME: 2 HOURS

PREPARATION

In a large bowl, mix the peanut butter, coconut oil, maple syrup, and sea salt. Pour the mixture into a parchment paper-lined loaf pan. Sprinkle chocolate chips over the top and freeze for two hours. Remove from the freezer and cut into squares.

NOTES

Store in the freezer as these will melt at room temperature!

INGREDIENTS

1 cup natural peanut butter
1/4 cup coconut oil
2 Tablespoons maple syrup
1/2 cup chocolate chips
1/2 teaspoon sea salt

Optional toppings:
Sea salt
Pretzels
Chopped walnuts
Coconut flakes

GLUTEN-FREE
VEGETARIAN

GUILT-FREE BROWNIES

We all need a pick-me-up here and there, and nothing says self-love like a warm batch of brownies. Change from your daytime pajamas into your nighttime ones, put on a facemask, and bake these ooey gooey brownies. You deserve it.

SERVES 9 | PREP TIME: 15 MINS | COOK TIME: 25 MINS

PREPARATION

Preheat oven to 350°F. Line an 8x8 inch pan with parchment paper or spray with non-stick cooking spray.

In a large bowl, mix together the wet ingredients. In a separate large bowl, whisk together the dry ingredients. Incorporate the dry ingredients into the wet ingredients and stir to combine. Pour the brownie batter into the pan and spread evenly.

Sprinkle some more chocolate chips on top and bake for 20-25 minutes. Let cool for 5-10 minutes. They will be super fudgey and will need to completely set before digging in. Cut into squares and enjoy!

INGREDIENTS

Wet:
2 eggs
1/3 cup maple syrup
1/3 cup coconut sugar
1/2 cup natural peanut butter
2 Tablespoons coconut oil, melted

Dry:
3/4 cup almond flour
1/2 cup cacao powder
1 teaspoon baking soda
1/4 teaspoon sea salt
1/2 cup chocolate chips

Optional toppings:
Chopped walnuts
Frosting
Sprinkles
Caramel
Sea salt
Raspberry jam

GLUTEN-FREE
VEGETARIAN

CHOCOLATE CHIP COOKIE SKILLET

It feels like years since we've been able to enjoy a delicious, warm dessert surrounded by friends at our favorite restaurant. I can't replace the friends, but I can replace the dessert with an even better homemade one. This airy, decadent cookie topped with your favorite ice cream is sure to make your night.

SERVES 4 | PREP TIME: 10 MINS | COOK TIME: 25 MINS

PREPARATION

Preheat oven to 350°F. Lightly grease an 8-inch cast iron skillet or nonstick pan.

In a medium microwave-safe bowl, warm the butter on high in 10 second intervals. Once the butter is melted, add brown sugar and granulated sugar to the bowl and mix until combined. Add the egg and vanilla, stirring until combined. Add flour, salt, and baking soda and stir until combined. Fold in the chocolate chips or chunks and spread the dough evenly into prepared skillet.

Bake for 20-25 minutes or until the edges are crispy and the center is set. Let cool slightly and serve warm with a big scoop of ice cream!

INGREDIENTS

1/4 cup unsalted butter
1/4 cup brown sugar
1/4 cup granulated sugar
1 egg
1 teaspoon vanilla extract
3/4 cup all-purpose flour
1/4 teaspoon baking soda
1/4 teaspoon sea salt
1/2 cup chocolate chips or chunks

Optional add-ins:
M&M's
Chopped peanut butter cups
Marshmallows
Toffee
Pretzels

CLASSIC NICE CREAM

I bet you didn't know you could make the yummiest soft-serve ice cream with just two staple ingredients! This no-churn banana "nice" cream is the perfect way to chill out after a stressful day... or year. This is the definition of a delicious, guilt-free treat!

SERVES 4 | PREP TIME: 15 MINS | REST TIME: 60 MINS

PREPARATION

Place frozen banana slices and almond milk into a high-speed food processor or blender. Blend on high for 1 to 2 minutes, stopping to scrape the sides every so often. If your blender is having a hard time, add more almond milk by the tablespoon.

Once pureed, your banana nice cream should have the consistency of a super thick smoothie or soft serve ice cream. Serve right away for a soft serve ice cream consistency or transfer to a parchment paper-lined loaf pan to freeze for later.

Freeze the nice cream for 1 to 2 hours so that it hardens enough to scoop like ice cream. When you're ready to eat set it out to thaw for 20 minutes before scooping and serving.

INGREDIENTS

Base Recipe:
4 cups frozen banana slices (about 2 large bananas)
2-4 Tablespoons almond milk

GLUTEN-FREE
DAIRY-FREE
VEGAN
VEGETARIAN

94

See next page for more.

NICE CREAM VARIATIONS

Personalize your nice cream with the following flavor combinations. The possibilities are endless! Simply follow the preparation instructions from the previous page.

Chocolate

Base nice cream recipe
1/2 cup unsweetened cacao powder
2 teaspoons vanilla extract

Chunky Monkey

Base nice cream recipe
1/3 cup dark chocolate chips
1/3 cup chopped walnuts

Mint Chocolate Chip

Base nice cream recipe
1/4 teaspoon mint extract
1/4 cup mini chocolate chips

Peanut Butter Cup

Base nice cream recipe
1-2 Tablespoons peanut butter
4 chopped peanut butter cups

Strawberry

Base nice cream recipe
(Substitute 1 cup frozen bananas for 1 cup frozen strawberries and use full-fat coconut milk)

Blueberry Cobbler

Base nice cream recipe
1 teaspoon vanilla extract
1/2 teaspoon ground cinnamon

Toppings:
1/4 cup of granola
3/4 cups fresh chopped blueberries.

index

Made in the USA
Columbia, SC
28 October 2020